What the Dickens?

Think you know the story of Scrooge backwards and forwards? Then you're in for some surprises--right along with Ebenezer. Writer/director Perry Waddell's production reinvents the famed holiday tale nightly. Tiny Tim as a alien? Scrooge, the victim of a mob boss? Bob Cratchit, a trekkie? Anything's possible when a show is one part faithful adaptation, three parts irreverent improvisation. Since audience suggestions guide how the spirits show the king of greed the error of his ways, you too have a major role in determining if this is a night to remember for more than just Scrooge.

—Julie Mehta, *Citysearch New York*

Scrooge's third Visitor.

Another Christmas Carol

A play written for improvisors by

Perry Waddell

from the story by Charles Dickens.

A scripted play, partly improvised from audience suggestions!

ANOTHER CHRISTMAS CAROL
www.AnotherChristmasCarol.com

Copyright © 2001 Perry Waddell

A part scripted/part improvised play from the story by Charles Dickens

All Rights Reserved

Professionals and amateurs are hereby warned that the performance of ANOTHER CHRISTMAS CAROL is subject to payment of royalty. It is fully protected under the copyright laws of the United States of America and of all countries covered by the International Copyright Union. All rights including professional/amateur stage rights, motion picture, recitation, lecturing, public reading, radio broadcasting, television, video, internet, animation, web cast, or sound recording, all other forms of mechanical or electronic reproduction such as CD-ROM, DVD, computers, data clouds, information storage and retrieval systems and photocopying, and the rights of translation into other languages are strictly reserved. Permission for any of the above must be secured from the author's agent in writing.

Performance rights for ANOTHER CHRISTMAS CAROL are controlled by THE LARVIK GROUP, LLC, POB 16, Ophir Oregon 97464. No professional or nonprofessional performance of the Play may be given without obtaining in advance the written permission of THE LARVIK GROUP, LLC, and paying the requisite fee.
For more information: www.AnotherChristmasCarol.com

SPECIAL NOTE

Anyone receiving permission to produce ANOTHER CHRISTMAS CAROL is required to give credit to the Author as sole and exclusive Author of the Play on the title page of all programs distributed in connection with performances of the Play and in all instances in which the title of the Play appears for purposes of advertising, publicizing or otherwise exploiting the Play and/or a production thereof. The name of the Author must appear in a separate line, in which no other name appears, immediately beneath the title and in size of type equal to 50% of the size of the largest, most prominent letter used for the title of the play. No person, firm or entity may receive credit larger or more prominent than that accorded the Author. The following acknowledgement must appear on the title page in all programs distributed in connection with performances of the Play:

"from the story by Charles Dickens"

Author   Perry Waddell
Cover images   Perry Waddell, Hood River Oregon USA
Interior Illustration   John Leech [Public domain], via Wikimedia Commons
Typography and Design   Perry Waddell
Font   Courier New 10
Printed by   CreateSpace, United States of America

Waddell, Perry
Another Christmas Carol: A Part Scripted, Part Improvised Play
From the story by Charles Dickens
Stage Play/Christmas/Holiday/Scrooge/Christmas Carol
1st printed ed.

ISBN: 1463688849
ISBN-13: 978-1463688844

TO

The Leather Pants Girl

FIRST PRODUCTION

ANOTHER CHRISTMAS CAROL was first produced off-off-Broadway at the GCI Theater (Dave Storck, Director) in New York City on November 30, 2001. The show takes approximately 60 minutes to perform. It was directed by Perry Waddell; the original music was by Stephen Couch; the lighting and sound design were by Perry Waddell; Martin Mitchell ran the booth; and Elizabeth Needham was the production assistant.

The cast was as follows:

Ebenezer Scrooge..David Thunder

Bob Cratchit...Myles Evans

Ghost of Marley..Arnold Rodriguez

Mrs. Cratchit / Lady...Beth Friedman

Ghost of Christmas Present...Clovis Douglas

A Boy / Gentleman..Dan Casto

Tiny Tim...Michele O. Medlin

Ghost of Christmas Past..Brian McMullan

Stage Manager..James 'Murf' Murphy

Ghost of Christmas Yet-To-Come.....................................Jody Kay

CONTENTS

Synopsis	vii
Cast	ix
Another Christmas Carol	1
Appendix	23
Scene Locations	24
Characters by Scene	25
Properties by Scene	26
Multimedia	27
Special Items	28
Cast - Scrooge	29
Cast - Bob Cratchit	31
Cast - Ghost of Marley	32
Cast - Mrs. Cratchit	34
Cast - Ghost of Christmas Past	36
Cast - A Boy/Gentleman	38
Cast - Tiny Tim	39
Cast - Ghost of Christmas Present	40
Cast - Stage Manager	41
Cast - Ghost of Christmas Future	42
Improvisation Tips	43
Improv 1 - Guide for Scene 3	44
Improv 2 - Guide for Scene 4	45
Improv 3 - Guide for Scene 5	46
Improvisation Sign-Up Sheets	47
Improv Sign-Up Sheet for Scene 3	48
Improv Sign-Up Sheet for Scene 4	50
Improv Sign-Up Sheet for Scene 5	52
About the Author	55

SYNOPSIS

Another Christmas Carol begins with the familiar scene in which Bob Cratchit sits at his desk freezing because his boss, Scrooge, a man whose name has become synonymous with miserly and stingy, will not allow him more coal for the stove. Mr. Scrooge is busy entering figures in a book when he is interrupted by carolers, whom he promptly chases off with threats of boiling water, then by charity workers who are chased off by the question, "Are there no more prison work houses?" It's a cold, dark, polluted and miserable day in London, and despite the extra burden of having Uncle Scrooge as his boss, Bob Cratchit remains in good spirits, even inviting his uncle for Christmas dinner.

Audiences know and love this story. They love to see Scrooge transformed into a new man. Another Christmas Carol invites the audience to help with the transformation by soliciting suggestions before the appearance of each ghost. The suggestions are incorporated into scenes improvised by the other actors. Audiences love to see how their suggestions are used in the stories of Scrooge's childhood and later life.

Actors love Another Christmas Carol because they can use their improv and acting skills to tie together the beginning and end of the play in as clever a way as possible. It is up to the actors to dramatize the audience suggestions so that the ghosts can easily explain the lessons that they are trying to teach Scrooge. The actor playing Scrooge can also direct the players by suggesting events such as, "Here is where I fell out of the tree" which the actors then have to perform.

After the opening scenes that demonstrate Scrooge's greediness, we go back to Scrooge's apartment. Here he is visited by the ghost of his deceased partner, Jacob Marley. Marley warns him of his fate should he continue his misguided ways and tells him he will be visited by three ghosts. An agitated and fearful Scrooge falls asleep before the ghosts arrive.

Next, the stage manager comes out and asks the audience to shout out holiday memories from their childhood. The stage manager then writes these down on sheets which are posted backstage, and the actors come out and create these scenes for the audience.

For the next ghost, this is repeated and the audience members can suggest ways in which they will be celebrating the holidays this year. Lastly, for the Ghost of Christmas Yet To Come, the audience members are asked to describe their greatest holiday dream for the future.

Once the ghosts have visited, Scrooge awakes to find that it is Christmas morning. Happy that it isn't too late to celebrate, Scrooge summons a child from the street and has him order the largest turkey from the butcher and have it delivered to the Cratchit family. Scrooge himself goes to the Cratchits' bearing gifts and notice of a salary increase for Bob. The play ends with Tiny Tim saying, "God bless us, every one".

Adapted from the original story, Another Christmas Carol uses some delightful, yet forgotten prose from Charles Dickens.

Cast

Cast is a minimum of 10 people.

Ebenezer Scrooge – Sole living owner of Scrooge & Marley

Bob Cratchit – Employee of Scrooge & Marley *and* nephew of Scrooge.

Ghost of Marley – Scrooge's long dead business partner.

Ghost of Christmas Past

Ghost of Christmas Present

Ghost of Christmas Future

Tiny Tim – Bob Cratchit's son.

A Boy – who is passing Scrooge's building on Christmas morning.

Mrs. Cratchit

Stage Manager

Gentleman – a charity worker.

Lady – a charity worker.

Cratchit Kids – 2 to 6 people

Perry Waddell

THE PLAY

Another Christmas Carol

STAGE MANAGER
Welcome to Another Christmas Carol. We have an exciting show planned for you but let me remind you, we need your help. We all know the story of that miser, that "Scrooge"! A stingy mean old man who doesn't appreciate anyone or anything besides money. Well, like Dickens, we want to teach him a lesson. So before each of the ghosts appears, I will come out and ask for your help in teaching Scrooge a lesson. Be ready to shout out your suggestions so we can convince Scrooge to love the holiday season.

FADE TO BLACK:

Scene: Scrooge's office -- AFTERNOON

(Lights up to find Scrooge sitting at a small desk upper S.R. He is writing in a ledger. Christmas carols play in the background. Scrooge grabs head.)

SCENE 1

SCROOGE
Bob! Bob! What's all that howling about? Are there dogs loose in the street?

(Bob enters from off stage, rubbing his hands to stay warm.)

BOB
It's carolers sir.

SCROOGE
What?

BOB
People are singing Christmas carols sir. They do it this time of year. People throw them pennies.

SCROOGE
Pennies do they? What nerve do they have coming around here singing about Christmas? Don't they know we are trying to work? I've got something to throw them- how about a kettle of boiling water? Send them away or I'll have them arrested!

(Bob leaves stage. Scrooge goes back to work then sets down his pen.)

SCROOGE (Continued)
Christmas, bah humbug!

(Bob enters, rubbing his shoulders to stay warm.)

BOB
What's that sir?

SCROOGE
I said humbug. Those carolers make me cross! How can I get any work done, living in this world of fools, breaking us down. When they all should let us be!

BOB
Yes sir.

SCROOGE
Holidays are just an excuse to be idle.

(Knock on the door)

SCROOGE (Continued)
Now what interruption? Get that Mr. Cratchit.

(Bob leaves stage and returns.)

BOB
A couple here to see you sir.

(Gentleman and lady enter)

GENTLEMAN
Scrooge and Marley's I believe? Do I have the pleasure of addressing Mr. Scrooge or Mr. Marley?

SCROOGE
Mr. Marley has been dead for seven years. He died seven years ago this very night.

LADY
I'm sorry sir.

SCROOGE
Sorry, why would you be sorry?

GENTLEMAN
Uh, I'm sure his generosity is represented well by his surviving partner.

LADY
At this festive time of year, Mr. Scrooge, it is more than usually desirable that we make some slight provision for the poor and destitute. There are those who suffer greatly at the present time. Many thousands are in want of common necessities; hundreds of thousands in need of common comforts, sir.

SCROOGE
Are there no prisons?

GENTLEMAN
Plenty of prisons sir.

SCROOGE
Are the union work houses still in operation?

GENTLEMAN
They are, still. I wish I could say they were not.

SCROOGE
Oh, I was afraid from what you said at first that something had happened- so glad to hear they are not closed. I would hate to have ruffians loose on the streets.

LADY
We represent an organization that helps these people get some meat, drink and warmth. We raise a fund to support this effort. We choose this holiday time because of all other times of the year, want is keenly felt and abundance rejoices. What shall I put you down for?

(Scrooge grabs head.)

SCROOGE
Nothing.

GENTLEMAN
You want to remain anonymous?

SCROOGE
I wish to be left alone! I don't make merry this time of year and can't afford to support others in their idleness. Those people can go to the work houses or to prison if they must.

LADY
Many can't go there.

GENTLEMAN
Some would rather die.

SCROOGE
Well die they should then... and get on with it. Reduce the surplus population. Their idleness is not my business. Bothering me with their Merry Christmas.

GENTLEMAN
But we are...

SCROOGE
It is enough for a man to understand his own business and to not interfere with other people's. Mine occupies me constantly and you sir and you madam are keeping me from it. Good afternoon!

(Scrooge goes back to his desk and picks up his pen. An embarrassed Bob shows the two visitors the door.)

SCROOGE (Continued)
Bob!

BOB
Yes, sir.

SCROOGE
Let no one else in. We have work to do. Next thing, more people will come around torturing us with their

(Scrooge makes quotes sign with his fingers.)
"Carols", man.

BOB
Well some people just wish to be merry, sir.

SCROOGE
Merry huh? Merry Christmas? What good has a Merry Christmas ever done you Bob?

BOB
Well...

SCROOGE
If I had my way, every person that runs around saying "Merry Christmas" would be boiled in his own pudding and with a stake of holly through his heart. He should!

BOB
It's a happy season sir.

SCROOGE
Happy season? Bah humbug. Who are you to talk about a happy season with 15 shilling a week and a wife and kids to boot. Why did you get married Cratchit?

BOB
Love, sir.

SCROOGE
Humbug Cratchit! Love. I've got something you can love. You got married so you would have an excuse to do less work. And I suppose you'll be wanting the whole day off tomorrow as well.

BOB
If quite convenient sir.

SCROOGE
It's not convenient!

BOB
It comes but once a year sir.

SCROOGE
Humbug! Is that any reason I should pay a day's wage without getting a day's work? A poor excuse for picking a man's pocket every 25th of December. I suppose you would feel ill used if I docked you 3 shillings for it.

(Scrooge paces around his desk while Bob looks anxiously on.)

BOB
May I have the day sir?

SCROOGE
Why so you can make merry?

BOB
Tiny Tim is counting on it sir.

SCROOGE
Bah! Hum... Well make sure you are here all the earlier the next morning. Understand? And make sure the fire is out and this place is tidy before you leave.

BOB
Thank you sir.

(Scrooge starts putting on his coat.)

BOB (Continued)
Oh, and sir?

SCROOGE
What is it man?

BOB
I wanted to invite you for Christmas dinner, Uncle Scrooge - that is if you don't already have plans.

SCROOGE
I'm too busy to make merry Cratchit. I will be working tomorrow.

(Scrooge exits. Bob pokes the fire, straightens out Scrooge's desk and quickly sweeps the floor-- then heads off stage.)

FADE TO BLACK:

SCENE 2

INT. Scrooge's Apartment -- NIGHT
(MARLEY, SCROOGE)

(Scrooge is sitting in a chair S.L. He is wearing his night clothes and is falling asleep with a ledger in his lap. He is startled awake.)

SCROOGE
What's that?

(Chains rattle off stage)

SCROOGE (Continued)
Is someone there?

(Scrooge looks around the room then settles back down. Sounds begin to be heard: bells then clanging then chains, footsteps etc... Scrooge becomes more and more terrified. The pale ghost of Marley enters S.L. dragging chains and carrying a candle. In a fright, Scrooge jumps from his chair and stands to face Marley.)

SCROOGE (Continued)
Who are you?

MARLEY
Ask me who I was.

SCROOGE
Who were you?

MARLEY
In life I was your partner, Jacob Marley.

SCROOGE
Marley!

(Scrooge falls backwards into his chair. He points to another chair.)

SCROOGE (Continued)
Can you sit down?

MARLEY
I can.
SCROOGE
Well, do it then.

MARLEY
You don't believe in me?

SCROOGE
I don't.

MARLEY
What evidence do you have of my reality beyond that of your senses?

SCROOGE
I don't know.

MARLEY
So then why do you doubt your senses?

(Scrooge feels his face and chest and slowly begins to stand up.)

SCROOGE
Because any little thing affects them: a slight disorder of the stomach makes them cheats. You may be nothing but an undigested bit of beef, a blot of mustard, a crumb of cheese, a fragment of an underdone potato, even yesterday's hot pocket. There's more of gravy than grave of you, whatever you are!

MARLEY
Scrooge, you unhappy man. I have come for you.

SCROOGE
But you have been dead for seven years! Seven years this night. Oh how I've missed you. Why have you come back?

MARLEY
Yes, I am dead- dead as a doornail! Though I, myself, would regard a coffin nail as the deadest piece of iron mongery in the trade, still, I will not disturb the wisdom of our ancestors in the simile. So therefore, I will repeat that yes, I am dead, dead as a doornail. But my spirit cannot rest. I have come to save you- save you from what I must endure.

(Scrooge stands.)

SCROOGE
Why? Our... my... but the business is doing well...

MARLEY
I have not come to save the business Scrooge, I've come to save you. In life I did not move among men and now, in death, there is only wandering, only wandering! Ohhhhhhhh!

SCROOGE
Surely there is some good. You were an upright businessman Marley, so handsome and debonair. You never hurt anybody.

MARLEY
Nor did I help them Ebenezer. Oh why did I shut my heart to people? Why did I turn my back on my fellow men and women? It was my wallet that ruled my life- I never listened to my heart- if even there was one there!
(feels chest)
Ohhhhhhhh!

SCROOGE
But we worked hard.

MARLEY
In life it got me only profit. In death... Ohhhhhhhh!

SCROOGE
So now you wander?

MARLEY
For me there is no rest, no peace, no quiet, no joy. I only wander, wander while pulling these chains. Incessant torture of remorse! Constant anguish of repentance. Continual cruciation of contriteness! Totally... Bad... Yuckky...

SCROOGE
Why are you chained?

MARLEY
These are the chains I forged in life. I made them- link by link, yard by yard. Would you know the length and weight of the strong coil you bear yourself? It was full and heavy as this, seven Christmas eves ago. Ebenezer you have labored on it since at a terrific rate. It is a ponderous chain!

(Scrooge looks down)

SCROOGE
I have chains?

MARLEY
Yes.

SCROOGE
Old Jacob Marley, tell me no more about the chains. Speak comfort to me!

MARLEY
I have none to give. The only thing I can tell you is that I am here to help you remove them link by link.

SCROOGE
But why should I get a chance when you got none?

MARLEY
Because I am your friend, your only friend Ebenezer. My spirit never walked beyond the counting house -- mark me! -- in life my spirit never roved beyond the narrow limits of our money changing hole. You have time to undo your chains. These chains that I built in life I cannot undo but by helping you,

I can lessen my own. By helping you, many of my links will be removed. You, my friend, would have done the same for me had you passed first.

SCROOGE
What must I do, Marley?

MARLEY
You, you can help us Ebenezer. If you listen, you can help us find peace. You must redeem your life before you die and you will redeem us both! If not, we will never have joy, never have contentment and you too will be forced to wander with no rest. Ohhhhhhhh!

(Scrooge quakes exceedingly)

SCROOGE
I will listen.

MARLEY
Listen and heed, Ebenezer.

SCROOGE
Yes, yes. What can I do?

MARLEY
You will be visited.

SCROOGE
What do you mean visited? I don't want any visitors. Marley you are the only visitor I would have.

(Scrooge reaches out to touch Marley but quickly pulls his hand back when he hears Marley mention 'ghosts'.)

MARLEY
You will be visited by three ghosts- three wandering spirits.

SCROOGE
No, no, no Marley! Don't send them! It's a ghost of an idea!

MARLEY
Expect the first spirit tonight when the bell tolls one.

SCROOGE
No, no!

MARLEY
Expect the second when the bell tolls two.

SCROOGE
Please Marley!

MARLEY
Expect the third when the bell tolls three.

SCROOGE
I will do anything you say Marley but please don't send them.

MARLEY
Without their visits, you cannot hope to shun the path I tread. Remember Ebenezer, listen to them and heed!

(Marley turns away from Scrooge and heads off stage dragging his chains. Scrooge stumbles back to his chair and sits down. Moaning heard in the distance slowly fades away. Scrooge looks up at the clock.)

SCROOGE
Two hours until a spirit arrives? Woe is me!

FADE TO BLACK:

SCENE 3

Ghost of Christmas Past -- MOMENTS LATER
(GHOST OF CHRISTMAS PAST, STAGE MANAGER, SCROOGE)

(Stage Manager enters and walks across very front of stage.)

STAGE MANAGER
Ladies and gentlemen, Scrooge has a cold heart. He does not remember that at one time it beat with laughter, joy and love. Yes, even love. We must show Scrooge something from his past and remind him of what he once was, what he is capable of being. Please someone give me a suggestion of a wonderful childhood memory. Something that happened to you, some event or occasion that brings back good memories for you.

(Stage Manager takes suggestion, makes sure it is clear and walks off stage.)

FADE TO BLACK:

(Lights come up to find Scrooge asleep in his chair. Scrooge is awakened by the sound of a bell tower tolling one.)

SCROOGE
What, what? Oh, the time has arrived!

(The Ghost of Christmas Past arrives and crosses stage. The Ghost stands next to the chair where Scrooge had been sleeping and looks down upon him.)

GHOST OF CHRISTMAS PAST
Ebenezer Scrooge!

SCROOGE
Yes, yes! Who are you? Why have you come?

GHOST OF CHRISTMAS PAST
I am the Ghost of Christmas Past.

SCROOGE
Long past?

GHOST OF CHRISTMAS PAST
No, your past Ebenezer.

SCROOGE
Marley told me of your coming. I asked him not to send you. Listen, if I could change my past I would definitely...

GHOST OF CHRISTMAS PAST
I've come to SHOW you your past. Nothing can be changed Ebenezer. I have little faith in this transformation. If you had a chance to live it again, I think nothing would change. You would do nothing differently Ebenezer.

SCROOGE
What of my past will you show me spirit?

GHOST OF CHRISTMAS PAST
Come with me.

SCROOGE
Some other time, perhaps. I have a bad back and indigestion.

GHOST OF CHRISTMAS PAST
Look Ebenezer...

(S.R. Lights up: improv here...)

Improv - audience suggests good memory of event from childhood. Ghost shows how good and nice Scrooge was as a child and how good many others were to him.

FADE TO BLACK

SCENE 4

Ghost of Christmas Present -- MOMENTS LATER
(ALL, GHOST OF CHRISTMAS PRESENT, STAGE MANAGER, SCROOGE)

STAGE MANAGER
So there was something warm in Scrooge's chest. I never knew that he... [refer to improv] Now we need to show Scrooge the joy of the present. We must teach him that despite their circumstances, people will do whatever they can to make merry on the holidays. Please, can someone tell me some specific way you will celebrate the holidays this year.

(Stage Manager takes suggestion, makes sure it is clear and walks off stage.)

FADE TO BLACK:

(Lights come up to find Scrooge sitting in his chair rocking back and forth and rubbing his hands. As the bell rings its second toll, all is quiet.)

SCROOGE
It is two o'clock.

(Silence off stage and on)

SCROOGE (Continued)
Where is my visitor? Spirit?

(Scrooge looks around and begins to get frantic)

SCROOGE (Continued)
Are you coming? Am I a lost cause already?

(Still no ghost)

SCROOGE (Continued)
Oh, this is worse than an actual visit! Spirit? Are you there?

(Ghost comes bursting through the doorway with a glass of wine and a half eaten donut.)

GHOST OF CHRISTMAS PRESENT
I'm sorry I am late old man. As I'm always living in the present, it's hard for me to keep appointments. Can't plan for the future- if you know what I mean. Would you like a donut?

(Scrooge, expecting a scary spirit, stares, mouth agape.)

GHOST OF CHRISTMAS PRESENT (Continued)
You have never seen the likes of me before?

SCROOGE
Never.

GHOST OF CHRISTMAS PRESENT
Every year another brother is born. Have you never walked forth with the younger members of my family. Never celebrated the holidays with my brothers?

SCROOGE
I don't think I have. I'm afraid I have not. Have you many brothers or sisters spirit?

(Ghost looks suspiciously at Scrooge)

GHOST OF CHRISTMAS PRESENT
More than eighteen hundred!

SCROOGE
A tremendous family to plan and provide for.

GHOST OF CHRISTMAS PRESENT
I am the Ghost of Christmas Present sir, there is no planning. I do what I want when I want for my time here on this place is very short. That's why I eat donuts and drink wine - or Absinthe. My arteries don't have time to clog.

SCROOGE
No moderation?

GHOST OF CHRISTMAS PRESENT
I overindulge in everything!

(Ghost finishes wine.)

SCROOGE
No savings?

GHOST OF CHRISTMAS PRESENT
I would spend it now.

(Ghost throws away donut.)

SCROOGE
No retirement plan?

GHOST OF CHRISTMAS PRESENT
Old shm-old! I live my life like there's no tomorrow!

SCROOGE
Spirit conduct me where you will, teach me what you have to but let's get this over with.

GHOST OF CHRISTMAS PRESENT
Touch my robe...

(S.R. lights up: improv here...)

Improv - audience suggestion of something they will do for the holidays. Ghost predicts how badly it will all turn out in order to scare Scrooge.

FADE TO BLACK:

SCENE 5

Ghost of Christmas Yet-To-Come -- MOMENTS LATER
(STAGE MANAGER, SCROOGE)

STAGE MANAGER
Now my favorite Ghost will appear. The strong, silent type. This Ghost can show us the future. Now again, we need help from you in the audience. We need to know about your dreams, your desires, your hopes for a wonderful life ahead. Tell me please, will you, a happy event, a gleeful occurrence, a

joyous occasion that you wish to happen in the future. Excellent, now let's show Scrooge.

(Stage Manager takes suggestion, makes sure it is clear and walks off stage.)

FADE TO BLACK:

(Lights come up to find Scrooge pacing. As the third toll hits, the Ghost of Christmas Yet-To-Come arrives slowly from off stage.)

SCROOGE
I have been shown the past and walked through the present. You must be the spirit of the future. The Ghost of Christmas Yet-To-Come. I fear you more than any other spirit I have seen.

(The Ghost points to stage right and offers his arm for Scrooge to hold.)

SCROOGE (Continued)
What are you going to show me?

(The Ghost does not reply. Reluctantly, Scrooge grabs the Ghost's arm and as he does, stage right is lighted.)

(S.R. lights up, improv the 'nightmare' here...)

Improv - audience suggestion of a dream for the future. We will turn it into a nightmare!

FACE TO BLACK

SCENE 6

INT. Scrooge's Apartment
(BOY, SCROOGE)

(Scrooge is asleep in the chair.)

SCROOGE
What, where am I?

(Scrooge gets up and looks around.)

SCROOGE (Continued)
Back home, my chair, the fireplace everything is here and... Oh Marley you said they would come and they did! They did come!... Oh what day is this?

(Scrooge goes to door, opens it and sees a young boy outside.)

SCROOGE (Continued)
Hey, there you. You boy. What day is this?

(Boy steps into doorway)

BOY
Why it's Christmas day.

SCROOGE
Yes, I didn't miss it.
(grabs face)
Oh this feels so good. I feel so good. They did it all in one night. Oh Marley!

(Turns to Boy)

SCROOGE (Continued)
The spirits did it all in one night!

BOY
Sir, are you drunk?

SCROOGE
Boy, do you know that poulterers around the corner?

BOY
I've lived my whole long glorious life here sir. I should hope I wasn't so dumb.

SCROOGE
Yes, yes, good fellow. Do you know if that prize turkey is still in the window?

BOY
The one that's as big as me?

SCROOGE
Yes, yes. What a boy you are; so bright, so handsome. It's a pleasure talking to you. Say, do you like Gladiators?

BOY
What are you on about old man?

SCROOGE
Oh, yes boy, I was coming to that. It's the big turkey I want! Yes, the one as big as you. Is it still there in the window?

BOY
Yes.

SCROOGE
Fine, fine! Go and order it for me and I'll give you a shilling.

BOY
What do you take me for? Is this a joke? I'm no ponce.

SCROOGE
Order it for me boy, tell the man to come along here. I will pay him for it and tell him where to deliver it. If you're back in five minutes I'll give you three shillings!

BOY
You got it!

(Boy runs off stage.)

SCROOGE
What a fine young boy and what a turkey! I say that it will be bigger than Tiny Tim. Cratchit won't know what to do with it. We will be eating like Royalty!

FADE TO BLACK:

SCENE 7

INT. The Living Room of Cratchit's Home -- AFTERNOON
(ALL, BOB, MRS. CRATCHIT, STAGE MANAGER, SCROOGE, TINY TIM)

(Lights up to find Bob, Mrs. Cratchit and Kids are sitting around the table talking and playing games.)

TINY TIM
Please tell us again about the Goose, mother!

MRS. CRATCHIT
Oh it's a fine juicy goose. Each of us will get half a potato and a nice sliver of goose. Then there will be gravy to pour over the top.

ALL
Yeah! Hooray!

BOB
Dear you are so resourceful.

TINY TIM
And the best mother ever!

BOB
Well said my boy!

ALL
Yes. Well Said. Thanks mum.

MRS. CRATCHIT
I say Bob, we will have a fine Christmas dinner.

TINY TIM
And don't forget the dessert.

ALL
Yeah. Yum. Desert. Pudding.

BOB
Don't worry crippled boy, none of us will forget the desert.

MRS. CRATCHIT
The pudding will be ready.

TINY TIM
What if, while we're eating, someone sneaks in and steals it.

ALL
Oh!

BOB
We'll lock the door!

TINY TIM
What if mice and rats sneak in under our feet and eat it?

MRS. CRATCHIT
The fire is too hot.

ALL
Yeah. Yeah.

TINY TIM
What if we all go deaf and blind and giant monkeys grab...

ALL
Shut up Tim! Stop it! I'm going to take your crutch!

MRS. CRATCHIT
Don't worry everybody, our dinner, including pudding for desert, will be just fine.

BOB
Yes, don't worry at all. I say we will have a fine meal.

MRS. CRATCHIT
Even though you work for the stingiest, most self-loathing...

BOB
Dear, the season!

MRS. CRATCHIT
I know dearest but the fact of the matter is that I think he can afford to pay you more than 15 shillings a week.

BOB
I do feel bad bringing home such a pittance to my family.

ALL
No father. No. It's fine. I'll be working soon...

MRS. CRATCHIT
Yes, I do appreciate that you have work when so many have none. But I still don't like Mr. Scrooge. Why I'd like to have him here right now! I'd give him a piece of my mind...

BOB
We should toast him tonight dear. I don't want to wish ill health on anyone- not even Mr. Scrooge.

MRS. CRATCHIT
Well, this is the holiday season and when it comes to the time when we drink our toasts, we will drink one for miserly Mr. Scrooge and his health just the same.

(There is a knock at the door.)

MRS. CRATCHIT (Continued)
Bob, are you expecting anyone?

BOB
Not on Christmas day dear.

(Mrs. Cratchit goes to the side of the stage and pulls back the curtain. Scrooge is just about to knock and instead steps inside.)

SCROOGE
Hello Mrs. Cratchit I hope I am not intruding.

(Startled, Bob jumps up from his chair and brushes off his clothes.)

BOB
Mr. Scrooge? Is anything wrong? Do I need to work today?

SCROOGE
No, no, Mr. Cratchit. I just came to wish you a Merry Christmas.

(All looked shocked.)

BOB AND MRS. CRATCHIT
A Merry Christmas?

SCROOGE
Yes and to tell you that the poulterer will be bringing your family a huge turkey- it should be here shortly.

MRS. CRATCHIT
A turkey?

SCROOGE
Yes and we'll have to get it in the oven right away so it will be ready for dinner. Could I be so bold as to accept your dinner invitation at this late time.

BOB
Why of course you can!

SCROOGE
Good, delightful, terrifically wonderful! And Mrs. Cratchit I took the liberty of bringing you these things from the market.

(Scrooge gives her a box of food stuffs but pulls out a bottle of wine before handing it over. He gives the bottle to Cratchit who opens it during the next few lines.)

TINY TIM
Mr. Scrooge are you drunk?

(Scrooge goes over to Tiny Tim and pinches his cheek.)

SCROOGE
Only with the joy of Christmas day my little cheeky monkey. And I have another box too. Presents for everyone!

(Scrooge grabs another box from outside the doorway.)

ALL
Ahhs and Ohhhs.

BOB
Have you gone mad Mr. Scrooge.

SCROOGE
Maybe... Yes, yes I have Bob. So mad that on my way over here, I left a note at the charity shop for that nice young couple to come over and collect a generous donation from me come Monday. So mad that our office will have enough coal to be as warm as a boy's bottom. So mad that young, adorable Tiny Tim there will be taken to a specialist for his lameness- at my expense! So mad right now, Bob Cratchit, that I want to make a toast to your salary.

(A puzzled Bob hands Mrs. Cratchit the wine. Mrs. Cratchit fills all glasses)

SCROOGE (Continued)
To Bob Cratchit. May he enjoy the raise he's going to be getting starting next week. Here's to 30 shillings a week!

BOB
Why that's twice...

SCROOGE
And to Mrs. Cratchit, little Tiny Tim and to all the Cratchit family.

(Bob looks at Mrs. Cratchit and urges her to pick up her glass.)

BOB
And to Mr. Scrooge.

MRS. CRATCHIT
Yes, Mr. Scrooge and his generosity.

ALL
Merry Christmas! Uncle Scrooge! Merry Christmas everybody!

(All turn to Tiny Tim.)

TINY TIM
And God bless us every one!

(All drink then bow to audience)

STAGE MANAGER
(Thank you, introduces cast who then sing a Christmas song)

# # #

Another Christmas Carol

Perry Waddell

Appendix

Scene Locations	24
Characters by Scene	25
Properties by Scene	26
Multimedia	27
Special Items	28
Cast - Scrooge	29
Cast - Bob Cratchit	31
Cast - Ghost of Marley	32
Cast - Mrs. Cratchit	34
Cast - Ghost of Christmas Past	36
Cast - A Boy/Gentleman	38
Cast - Tiny Tim	39
Cast - Ghost of Christmas Present	40
Cast - Stage Manager	41
Cast - Ghost of Christmas Future	42
Improvisation Tips	43
Improv 1 - Guide for Scene 3	44
Improv 2 - Guide for Scene 4	45
Improv 3 - Guide for Scene 5	46
Improvisation Sign-Up Sheets	47
Improv Sign-Up Sheet for Scene 3	48
Improv Sign-Up Sheet for Scene 4	50
Improv Sign-Up Sheet for Scene 5	52

Scene Locations

SCENE ONE: Scrooge's office. Afternoon before Christmas Eve.

SCENE TWO: Scrooge's sitting room on stage left. Christmas evening.

SCENE THREE: Scrooge's sitting room on stage left, improv on stage right. Improvs take place that night and then years in the past.

SCENE FOUR: Scrooge's sitting room on stage left, improv on stage right. Improvs take place in time later that night and near future.

SCENE FIVE: Scrooge's sitting room on stage left, improv on stage right. Improvs take place in time even later that night and then in the future.

SCENE SIX: Scrooge's sitting room on stage left. Christmas day morning.

SCENE SEVEN: Bob Cratchit's house. Christmas day.

Another Christmas Carol

Characters in each scene

("Assorted players" parts performed by improv team)

SCENE ONE: Scrooge, Bob, Gentleman, Lady, Stage Manager.

SCENE TWO: Scrooge Ghost of Marley.

SCENE THREE: Scrooge, Ghost of Christmas Past, Assorted Players, Stage Manager.

SCENE FOUR: Scrooge, Ghost of Christmas Present, Assorted Players, Stage Manager.

SCENE FIVE: Scrooge, Ghost of Christmas Yet-To-Come, Assorted Players, Stage Manager.

SCENE SIX: Scrooge, Boy.

SCENE SEVEN: Scrooge, Bob, Mrs. Cratchit, Tiny Tim and Kids, Stage Manager.

Properties in each scene

SCENE ONE: Scrooge's desk with ledger, pen and ink well. Chair. Coat rack.

SCENE TWO: Scrooge's sitting chair, ledger, left-over food in bowl, teacup, and a fireplace or mantle on wall.

SCENE THREE: Same as Two plus any items needed for improv.

SCENE FOUR: Same as Two plus any items needed for improv.

SCENE FIVE: Same as Two plus any items needed for improv.

SCENE SIX: Same as Two.

SCENE SEVEN: Table, chairs, glasses, juice, wine. Box of foods, box of assorted Christmas presents.

Multimedia

SCENE ONE: Full lights. No sounds.

SCENE TWO: Lights stage left. Sounds of chains, rattles, knocks, cries, footsteps.

SCENE THREE: Lights stage left switch to stage right for improv. Strobe for Ghost's arrival. Sounds of church bells chime and stroke of one o'clock.

SCENE FOUR: Lights stage left switch to stage right for improv. Sounds of church bells chime and stroke of two o'clock.

SCENE FIVE: Lights stage left switch to stage right for improv. Strobe for Ghost's arrival. Sounds of church bells chime and stroke of three o'clock.

SCENE SIX: Full lights. Birds singing.

SCENE SEVEN: Light Christmas music, full lights.

Special Items Needed

Sounds

-chains

-clock chimes with stroke of one, two and three o'clock bells.

-bird singing

Props

-fireplace or mantle or stove

-chair

-ledger

-ink well and quill pen

-coat rack

Costumes

-chains

CAST

Ebenezer Scrooge

Scrooge is the stingy, mean old miser who is only concerned with money. We see, through this story, his transformation to a warm and generous gentleman.

Costume:

- Scene One - Old fashioned business suit
- Scene Two through Six - Dressing Gown with cap
- Scene Seven - Business suit

Props:

- Scene One - Pen and ledger
- Scene Two through Six - Candle
- Scene Six - Coin
- Scene Seven - Box of food, box of presents

Appearances:

- All scenes

Description by Charles Dickens:
"Oh! But he was a tight-fisted hand at the grindstone, Scrooge! a squeezing, wrenching, grasping, scraping, clutching, covetous, old sinner! Hard and sharp as flint, from which no steel had ever struck out generous fire; secret, and self-contained, and solitary as an oyster. The cold within him froze his old features, nipped his pointed nose, shriveled his cheek, stiffened his gait; made his eyes red, his thin lips blue; and spoke out shrewdly in his grating voice. A frosty rime was on his head, and on his eyebrows, and his wiry chin. He carried his own low temperature always about with him; he iced his office in the dogdays; and didn't thaw it one degree at Christmas.

External heat and cold had little influence on Scrooge. No warmth could warm, no wintry weather chill him. No wind that blew was bitterer than he,

no falling snow was more intent upon its purpose, no
pelting rain less open to entreaty. Foul weather didn't
know where to have him. The heaviest rain, and
snow, and hail, and sleet, could boast of the advantage
over him in only one respect. They often `came down'
handsomely, and Scrooge never did.

Nobody ever stopped him in the street to say, with
gladsome looks, `My dear Scrooge, how are you?
When will you come to see me?' No beggars implored
him to bestow a trifle, no children asked him
what it was o'clock, no man or woman ever once in all
his life inquired the way to such and such a place, of
Scrooge. Even the blind men's dogs appeared to
know him; and when they saw him coming on, would
tug their owners into doorways and up courts; and
then would wag their tails as though they said, `No
eye at all is better than an evil eye, dark master!'

But what did Scrooge care! It was the very thing
he liked. To edge his way along the crowded paths
of life, warning all human sympathy to keep its distance,
was what the knowing ones call `nuts' to Scrooge."

CAST

– Bob Cratchit

– Improv player - additional role.

Bob is Scrooge's underpaid, under appreciated (and freezing cold) clerk. He is afraid to stand-up to Scrooge as he feels lucky to have any job at all. Usually gets by through hard work and generally agreeing with his boss. A poor, mild man, he is happy in his life because of his love for his wife and family. At home with his family is the place he experiences his real joy for life- despite his worries for the health of Tiny Tim. In this version, Bob Cratchit is also Scrooge's nephew.

Costume:

- Scene One - Cheap business suit, hat, fingerless gloves
- Scene Three-Five - shirt and slacks
- Scene Seven - Cheap business suit

Props:

- Scene One - Pen and ledger
- Scene Seven - Wine glass

Appearances:

- Scene One - Bob Cratchit
- Scenes Three, Four, Five - Improv Player
- Scene Seven - Bob Cratchit

CAST

– Ghost of Marley

- **Improv player - additional role.**
- **Cratchit child - additional role.**

The Ghost of Marley is a tortured soul. He feels very sorry for himself and likes to ramble on and listen to himself speak.

Costume:
- Scene Two - Business suit, powdered hair
- Scene Three, Four, Five - Shirt and slacks
- Scene Seven - Tattered shirt and trousers

Props:
- Scene Two - Chains and locks

Appearances:
- Scene Two - Ghost of Marley
- Scenes Three, Four, Five - Improv Player
- Scene Seven - Cratchit Kid

Description by Dickens:
"The same face: the very same. Marley in his pigtail,
usual waistcoat, tights and boots; the tassels on
the latter bristling, like his pigtail, and his coat-skirts,
and the hair upon his head. The chain he drew was
clasped about his middle. It was long, and wound
about him like a tail; and it was made (for Scrooge
observed it closely) of cash-boxes, keys, padlocks,
ledgers, deeds, and heavy purses wrought in steel.
His body was transparent; so that Scrooge, observing him,
and looking through his waistcoat, could see
the two buttons on his coat behind.

Another Christmas Carol

Scrooge had often heard it said that Marley had no
bowels, but he had never believed it until now.

No, nor did he believe it even now. Though he
looked the phantom through and through, and saw
it standing before him; though he felt the chilling
influence of its death-cold eyes; and marked the very
texture of the folded kerchief bound about its head
and chin, which wrapper he had not observed before;
he was still incredulous, and fought against his senses."

CAST

– Mrs. Cratchit

- **Lady - additional role (for smaller cast).**
- **Improv player - additional role.**

Mrs. Cratchit is sincere, hard working and totally in love with Bob and her family. Though the Cratchits are of little means, Mrs. Cratchit manages to use her intelligence to make every penny go as far as possible and to help her family always be happy and content. She also totally despises Mr. Scrooge.

Lady is a proper but dear woman who works on behalf of charity. Her husband is "Gentleman".

Costume:

- Scene One – Business attire and long coat
- Scene Three, Four, Five – Slacks and Shirt
- Scene Seven – Tattered dress

Props:

- Scene One – Clipboard, pen and envelope
- Scene Seven – Kitchen supplies? Corkscrew.

Appearances:

- Scene One - Lady
- Scene Three, Four, Five – Improv Player
- Scene Seven – Mrs. Cratchit

Description by Dickens:
"Then up rose Mrs. Cratchit, Cratchit's wife, dressed out but poorly in a twice-turned gown, but brave in ribbons, which are cheap and make a goodly show for sixpence;
…
`Why, bless your heart alive, my dear, how late you are.'
said Mrs Cratchit, kissing her a dozen times, and taking off her shawl and bonnet for her with officious zeal.
…
There was nothing of high mark in this. They were not a handsome family; they were not well dressed; their shoes were far from being water-proof; their clothes were scanty;

and Peter might have known, and very likely did, the inside of a pawnbroker's. But, they were happy, grateful, pleased with one another, and contented with the time; and when they faded, and looked happier yet in the bright sprinklings of the Spirit's torch at parting, Scrooge had his eye upon them, and especially on Tiny Tim, until the last."

CAST

- Ghost of Christmas Past

- **Improv Player - additional role.**
- **Cratchit Kid - additional role.**

The Ghost of Christmas Past is a strong yet delicate creature. This is the most important Ghost as he has much to show Scrooge and sets the stage for how the spirit visits will work. Therefore, he takes his role very seriously and is quick to offend.

Costume: Long robe

Props: none

Appearances:

- Scene Three - Ghost of Christmas Past
- Scene Four - Improv Player
- Scene Five - Improv Player
- Scene Seven - Cratchit Kid

Tricks:

When Scrooge tries to interact with what he sees in the improv scene, the Ghost says:

`These are but shadows of the things that have been,' said the Ghost. `They have no consciousness of us.'

Description by Dickens:
"It was a strange figure -- like a child: yet not so like a child as like an old man, viewed through some supernatural medium, which gave him the appearance of having receded from the view, and being diminished to a child's proportions. Its hair, which hung about its neck and down its back, was white as if with age; and yet the face had not a wrinkle in it, and the tenderest bloom was on the skin. The arms were very long and muscular; the hands the same, as if its hold were of uncommon strength. Its legs and feet, most delicately formed, were, like those upper members, bare. It wore a tunic of the purest white, and round its waist was bound a lustrous belt, the sheen of which was beautiful. It held a branch of fresh green holly in its hand; and, in singular

contradiction of that wintry emblem, had its dress trimmed with summer flowers. But the strangest thing about it was, that from the crown of its head there sprung a bright clear jet of light, by which all this was visible; and which was doubtless the occasion of its using, in its duller moments, a great extinguisher for a cap, which it now held under its arm."

CAST

— A Boy
- **Gentleman** - additional role (for smaller cast).
- **Improv player** - additional role.
- **Cratchit Boy** - additional role.

A Boy is the smarmy, smart-alec little kid who is walking by Scrooge's flat on Christmas day.

Gentleman is a charity collector.

Costume:

- Scene One - Business suit and long coat
- Scene Three, Four, Five - Slacks and Shirt
- Scene Six - Boy clothes: shirt and trousers and cap. Rosy cheeks a plus.
- Scene Seven - Cratchit kid

Props:

- none

Appearances:

- Scene One - Gentleman
- Scene Three, Four, Five - Improv Player
- Scene Six - A Boy
- Scene Seven - Cratchit kid

CAST

— Tiny Tim

- **Improv player - additional role.**

Tiny Tim is the sweet little son of Bob and Mrs. Cratchit. Tim suffers from an illness or handicap. We all know Tim.

Costume:

- Scene Three, Four, Five – Slacks and Shirt
- Scene Seven – Osh Kosh Bibs or other boyish clothes

Props:

- Scene Seven – Crutch

Appearances:

- Scene Three, Four, Five – Improv Player
- Scene Seven – Tiny Tim

CAST

- Ghost of Christmas Present

- **Improv player - additional role.**
- **Cratchit kid - additional role.**

Hedonist. Lover of food and drink, this spirit is the cheekiest of all. Because he is living for the moment, he is the least responsible of the ghosts and also has the most fun as he doesn't take his role as seriously as the other two. Tough at the end when it is time to teach Scrooge a lesson, he gets very serious. Very flamboyant, flowing with life and often distracted by his own indulgences.

Costume: Toga or robe with green leaf crown (or similar). Sandals.

Props: Glass with a little bit of wine and a half eaten donut.

Appearances:

1. Scene Three - Improv Player
2. Scene Four - Ghost of Christmas Present
3. Scene Five - Improv Player
4. Scene Seven - Cratchit Kid

Character Described by Dickens:
"It was clothed in one simple green robe, or mantle, bordered with white fur. This garment hung so loosely on the figure, that its capacious breast was bare, as if disdaining to be warded or concealed by any artifice. Its feet, observable beneath the ample folds of the garment, were also bare; and on its head it wore no other covering than a holly wreath, set here and there with shining icicles. Its dark brown curls were long and free; free as its genial face, its sparkling eye, its open hand, its cheery voice, its unconstrained demeanour, and its joyful air. Girded round its middle was an antique scabbard; but no sword was in it, and the ancient sheath was eaten up with rust."

CAST

– Stage Manager

The Stage Manager is the M.C. of the entire performance. Not only does the Stage Manger introduce the show, most importantly, he also gets the suggestions from the audience.

It is up to him to make sure the audience's suggestions are well understood and specific yet general enough for actors to improv.

Costume:
- Nice suit, prefer 3-piece

Props:
- Pipe or cane

Appearances:
- Scene One – intro play
- Scene Three, Four, Five – intro each
- Scene Seven – End of show – do introductions, thank you.

CAST

– Ghost of Christmas Yet-To-Come
- **Improv player - additional role.**
- **Cratchit child - additional role.**

The Ghost of Christmas Yet-To-Come is the scariest of all the Ghosts. She does not speak but merely leads and observes. Scrooge is at his worst with her as her silence only adds to his nervousness. She is strong and grand.

Costume:
- Scene Three-Four – Slacks and Shirt
- Scene Five – Medieval gold dress
- Scene Seven – Tattered shirt and trousers

Props:
- None

Appearances:
- Scene Three-Four – Improv Player
- Scenes Five – Ghost of Christmas Yet-To-Come
- Scene Seven – Cratchit Kid

Description by Dickens:
"The Phantom slowly, gravely, silently approached. When it came, Scrooge bent down upon his knee; for in the very air through which this Spirit moved it seemed to scatter gloom and mystery.
…
He felt that it was tall and stately when it came beside him, and that its mysterious presence filled him with a solemn dread. He knew no more, for the Spirit neither spoke nor moved."

Improvisation Tips

In General:

-Justify, justify, justify.

-Label people quickly.

-Make sure the scenes become lessons.

-Scrooge and Ghost will walk around as they are observing. Leave space for dialog from Scrooge and Ghost.

-Do NOT interact with Scrooge or Ghost in any way.

-Do not wear the same costume when improvising that your character wears.

-LISTEN to what Scrooge and the Ghost say. Scrooge may say "this is where I fell down". Whoever is playing Scrooge now HAS to fall down.

-Editing and cutting scenes is encouraged.

-GHOSTS should bring in Scrooge's lines from scene one to haunt him. ("Yes, Scrooge, reduce the surplus population...")

-Maybe bring in characters (Oliver) or lines ("these were the best of times, these were the worst of times") from other Dickens stories.

-The GHOST will end the scene and lead Scrooge back to stage left which is his bedroom. Lights and sound will follow by darkening stage right.

-The goal of each improvisation is to teach Scrooge a lesson and to help him, slowly, transform from the miser he is to a generous, kind and giving person. In his youth, Scrooge saw and knew people like this and the actors can show him examples.

-Let Scrooge and the Ghost take a major lead in directing the scene and also defer to their dialog throughout.

-Improv actors do not interact with Scrooge or the Ghost in any way.

-Ghost will edit and end improv. Lights will follow.

-Take SIMPLE and GENERAL suggestions from the audience.

Improv 1- Ghost of Christmas Past
(Scene 3: 15-18 minutes)

IMPROVS:

We will take 3 suggestions from the audience.

The first scene will be Scrooge as a child, the second will be Scrooge as a kid/teenager and the third will be Scrooge as a young man.

Lesson: To show Scrooge that there was a time when he had joy, love and warmth in his heart. And to show him that others who celebrated Christmas, even in a minor way, could bring much happiness to themselves and others.

Story: In Dickens's story, Scrooge is first shown his childhood, his friends and how his sister came and saved him from the orphanage. Next he is shown the office where he apprenticed. There, he sees the joy his boss, Fezziweg, brought him and his colleague as Fezziweg throws a wonderful party for the company's Christmas. Scrooge comments on how Fezziweg could bring joy to their hearts. Last, the Ghost shows Scrooge what happens when Scrooge's girlfriend leaves him cause all he cares about anymore is money. Scrooge is yelling at his younger self to "talk to her" and then Scrooge weeps.

Improv Tricks:

-The same person should play the younger Scrooge here in all three scenes to prevent audience confusion.

-Scrooge may label people as he recognizes them, "Oh there's funny Eddie!"

-Scrooge should try to interact with the players early in this scene. When he does, the Ghost says:

`These are but shadows of the things that have been,' said

the Ghost. `They have no consciousness of us.'

Improv 2- Ghost of Christmas Present
(Scene 4: 10-12 minutes)

IMPROVS:

We will take 3 suggestions from the audience.

The Cratchit family will be in one. The other two (short) improv scenes will show ways that others with little means celebrate Christmas. They do not have to be in any particular order.

Lesson: To show Scrooge that other people do what they can with little means they have to celebrate Christmas. Even though he is Scrooge, people still toast him and feel sorry for him and feel sorry for what Scrooge is missing.

Story: In Dickens's story, Scrooge is shown the Cratchit family and their meager table. Then he sees them drink a toast to Scrooge, with some objections, despite the fact he is so mean and stingy with Cratchit. Scrooge learns of Tiny Tim and asks if he will live. The Ghost says he sees an empty chair. They also go to a factory and a ship at sea and see that people all over the world, of every means and in every occupation and doing what they can to celebrate the holiday season.

Improv Tricks:

-Scene should be about Cratchit family and/or others who know Scrooge.

-Can also bring in other strange groups of characters that are celebrating in their own way.

Improv 3- Ghost of Christmas Yet-To-Come
(Scene 5: 10-12 minutes)

IMPROVS:

We will take 2 suggestions.

In one, TINY TIM must die. In the other, SCROOGE must die.

Lesson: We will take audiences suggestion of something good and change it into a nightmare to teach Scrooge that if he doesn't change his evil ways, this is what fate has in store for him. Probably should be something horrible that results in Scrooge's death.

Story: In Dickens's story, Scrooge is warned that he will die soon and no one will be sad or care. In contrast, some people will even look to profit from it. Also, maybe he could have gotten help if there was someone in his life that cared for him.

Scrooge is first shown some stock exchange gentlemen talking about someone who died. He is also shown servants selling his things and a corpse covered in a sheet. He keeps asking the ghost who the person is that died and in the last scene, Scrooge is put in a cemetery where he turns and sees his own name on the gravestone. At the end, Scrooge asks if these events are unavoidable: "I know that if a man's actions change so do his ends." Then he realizes, "why show me this (ghost,) if I have passed all hope?!"

Improv Tricks:

-Remember this Ghost never speaks, only leads.

-Don't label the improv actor who is Scrooge. Let the real Scrooge try to figure out who the person is who is dying.

-We will get from the audience, something GOOD that they hope will happen. One of their DREAMS for the future. In the improv, we will turn it into a **NIGHTMARE**! Just like the nightmare improv game.

Improvisation
Sign-Up Sheets

-Before the show, write the cast member's name (who is playing that particular ghost) in the space for each of the three ghosts.

-Also before the show, cast members (not the ghost for that scene or Scrooge) sign-up for each of the improv roles. Sign your name next to a character name (i.e. "Scrooge" or "Tiny Tim") and then you will play that character in the improv.

-When the stage manager gets the three or two suggestions each time he appears on stage, he writes them in the spaces (1., 2., 3...) and **posts** the sheet backstage.

-If there is no character name next to the sign-up line, then you can play any character that the improv dictates.

Improv Sign-Up Sheet for Scene 3

Ghost of Christmas Past Actor's Name: _____

Audience Suggestions:

1. _____

2. _____

3. _____

Improv actor playing Scrooge for all three scenes-

Actor's name: _____

Improv 1- Scrooge as a child

Show how kind people were to Scrooge and how kind he was in return.

Improv actor: _____

Improv actor: _____

Another Christmas Carol

Sign-Up Sheet for Scene 3, Page 2

Improv 2- Scrooge as a teenager

Show how kind people were to teenage Scrooge and how kind he was in return.

Improv actor:_____

Improv actor:_____

Improv 3- Scrooge as a Young man

Scrooge starts to become greedy, stingy, only caring about money...

Improv actor:_____

Improv actor:_____

Improv Sign-Up Sheet for Scene 4

Ghost of Christmas Present Actor's Name: _____

Audience Suggestions:

1. _____

2. _____

3. _____

Improv 1- Cratchit Christmas

Show how the Cratchit family happily celebrates with very little means.

Mr. Cratchit: _____

Mrs. Cratchit: _____

Tiny Tim _____

Improv actors:(Optional) _____

_____

Sign-Up Sheet for Scene 4, Page 2

Improv 2- Others celebrate and toast Scrooge

Show how people who don't like Scrooge and maybe owe him money, still toast him.

Improv actor: _____

Improv actor: _____

Improv actor: _____

Improv 3- Others, with little means celebrate Christmas

Anyone can celebrate, it doesn't take cash or wealth…

Improv actor: _____

Improv actor: _____

Improv actor: _____

Improv Sign-Up Sheet for Scene 5

Ghost of Christmas Future Actor: _____

Audience Suggestions:

1. _____

2. _____

Improv 1- Tiny Tim dies

Tim dies cause they have no money or no doctor. Attribute to Cratchits being poor.

Tiny Tim: _____

Improv actor: _____

Improv actor: _____

Improv actors:(Optional) _____

_____

Another Christmas Carol

Sign-Up Sheet for Scene 5, Page 2

Improv 2- Scrooge dies

Scrooge has no one to care for him, too mean and stingy, he never looked after himself or anyone else.

Scrooge: _____

Improv actor: _____

Improv actor: _____

Improv actors:(Optional) _____

_____

_____

_____

ABOUT THE AUTHOR

Perry Waddell is an attorney in Brooklyn, New York where he lives with his wife and son. He studied writing at New York University, theater at Stella Adler Acting School and improvisational comedy at Gotham City Improv. He is the author of a short story collection, a book of poetry, multiple scripts for television and film and is writing a novel. Waddell was a founding member of the infamous New York City improvisational comedy troupe *pembo!*

Made in the USA
Charleston, SC
15 July 2011